SIGNAL BOOKS SIGNATURE POETS SERIES

THE LIGHT BETWEEN THE FIELDS

Christopher Brookhouse

Library of Congress Cataloging-in-Publication Data

Brookhouse, Christopher, 1938-
  The light between the fields / Christopher
Brookhouse
    p. cm. — (Signal Books signature poets series)
  ISBN 0-930095-34-0
  I. Title. II. Series.
PS3552.R658L55 1998
811'.54—dc21   98-19403
                                              CIP

for Cy and A.P.

ACKNOWLEDGMENTS

Earlier versions of "6 A.M.," "The Witch," "Hilda and the Snakes," "Wintering," "Jackson Pollock," and "The Finding" appeared in *Scattered Light*.

Earlier versions of "An Old Irish Woman," "On Jack's Birthday," "For Stephen," "1945–," and "Reply" appeared in *Carolina Quarterly*.

An earlier version of "Burial" appeared in *Agenda*.

An earlier version of "Tourists" appeared in *New Southern Writing*.

"The Reverend B.E. Palmer Considers his Harvest," "When Someone in our Country Parish Died," "Vespers," and "Remedy" appeared in *The Sewanee Review*.

"Tonight" appeared in *Asylum*.

"Elegy" appeared in *Colby-Sawyer Alumni Magazine*.

"Ohio, Knox County, September" appeared in *The Gettysburg Review*, which also published *The Planned Child* under the title *Self Story*.

CONTENTS

ELEGY

A Sunday at September's end.
Under the turning leaves a thin
Light fingers the slender grass.

I stand at a window with the dead.
The air smells sweet from limes and gin.
I stood here fifty years ago.

The war was over then. The guests
Squeezed into their luminous skins,
The ones without badges or grief.

It was a party afternoon.
A time to let forgetting begin,
A time to turn off clocks.

It was an afternoon to consume
Lobsters, corn on the cob, and gin,
An afternoon to taste and see

The ways light moved around the room,
To feel shadows cross the skin
And not to think of any dying,

Not to encounter any dismay
For all the brightness growing thin
Across the lawns, the cars, the houses.

I was a child then. A woman
Put her mouth near mine and said,
No forgetting can begin
Without permission from the dead.

REPLY

Here among spruce and birch, in the mountain's shadow,
unknot memory, ease your dead father down
to splays of feldspar and fern — he lives again,

crossing his flannel arms, looking off.
Once you asked what he saw. A bear, he answered,
fat from berries, dancing the season's farewell.

Scanning the mountain, you perceived nothing,
certainly not the vast dark settling in.
Now as you lean against rocks, your own son

Watching you, let him repeat the question —
already you have gone out of your body, dancing
the ghost bear's joy, the shared summoning.

REMEDY

I'm fading. The first cold winds unwind
Me from my summer skin and turn me out.

Ah summer, the fix. I wore you like make-up.
You toned each muscle's line.
Evenings I flexed before the soul's mirror,
Believing I had the strength for pain.
Outside I would age like Cary Grant.

One day pain surprised me, a twinge
Through the gut at first, then bouts
That used me up like a ruthless lover.
My cock shrivels. My balls are stones.
My kidneys swell the size of cantaloupes.

Tap, tap, tap the doctor plays them.
The hall sours with men drooping in chairs.
Get in line, the doctor says.
My heart does its cha-cha-cha of fear.

II

Yes . . . so . . . the winter unwinds us.
Count it blessing.
Find a plainer style.
Lullaby of simple things.

See how the leaves blow away.
The roads reappear among the hills.
The world opens.
The deeper you go into it,
The smaller you become.

You forget who you wanted to be,
And where you hurried to go.
Space and cold have their mercies.
Pain opens its hand.
You step out.
Under the moon you bow to your shadow.
You slow dance in your pale, new skin.

ARGUMENT

You're a bitch, husband said.
You're a bastard, wife said.
Each offered evidence.
Thus they argued, back
To back, word to word,
Pretending to change for supper.

Both kept shouting
On the way to town in the
Minivan, their two wide-
Eyed children belted into
Kids' space, extolled in ads
Where glossy couples conveyed
Children, plus Dalmatian, to
Little League and ballet.
Fields gave way to fences.
By the time the van reached
Town, the children huddled
In each other's arms, skins
Wet with tears. Wet
With tears they all were.

Husband pulled over.
In the van he sat weeping more.
Wife wept more. Children wept more.
A young boy passing by then decided
To have a peek, perhaps to examine

Kids' space for himself or else the dog.
The husband, who had curious
Religious inclinations for late
In the century, despite
Falling into the 7 deadlies
On a regular basis . . .
The husband found a face
Pressed against the glass,
Flat lips, white nose,
Small round, dark eyes.
The husband laughed.
The wife laughed.
The children laughed.

The boy didn't. He kept
His face pressed to the glass
Until the van rocked inside out.
The husband opened the door,
Asked the boy his name. Mike,
The kid said. Michael,
The husband thought, and though
Mike didn't appear in any
Sort of angel outfit,
The husband knew better.

The boy wandered off.
The husband embraced his wife.
The wife embraced her husband.
The children complained they were hungry.
At the restaurant the family dined

With friends. Everyone selected
The foods they ordered every week.
Look at us, one friend said;
If anything out of the ordinary
Happened we'd be scared to death.
On Wednesdays I always order catfish.
It always tastes the same.

So friends went about their meals
Except the husband. He was thinking
About the ordinary, the great familiar
Surrounding us, how it comes apart
Sometimes, how no secrets are hid.
There in the middle of the table
You can see the heart of the dead fish beating,
You can see the glory on the skins of peoples' faces,
You can see light speeding over everything
Because on the roadside a messenger opened your eyes.

WHEN SOMEONE IN OUR COUNTRY PARISH DIED

When someone in our country parish died
the good girls learned to bake the funeral pies.
Instead I patted out the smeary dough
And traced the warning head, the skull smooth
As a three-way bulb, thumbed holes for eyes,
And gave the mouth a little pout,
Then forefingered in
    the bowtie of bones
        crossed beneath the chin.

My own mother died the winter I turned fifteen,
In cold so deep the diggers' spades broke.
Stiff and washed she bided in the parlor.
The room still smelled of Christmas evergreen.
I offered death cookies and a coke,
Then argued guilt
    with the gray face
        floating on its quilt.

At last we bore her from the house, a day
So cold no one remembered worse. The shoe
Which paced the grave's dimensions off lacked
Two feet of being true. Men sent away
For dynamite, set the caps, and blew
Cusps of grass up, dangling root.
    They filled the air
        like models of a wisdom tooth.

No wisdom in me though. At home the men
Shared whiskey while we women made the meal.
I stole a bottle for myself and drank
Until the cold came off, then my skin,
And disarrayed in my best bones I reeled
From hand to hand, from face to face,
    until I stood at last
        empty, obedient, in place.

THINKING OF MARGARET

That Easter at the country club
I dressed in blue to hunt for eggs.
I found the prize one near the dogwoods.
Margaret Hartley said she'd kiss me for it.
I wasn't interested.
                          The sky had clouded over.
Wings of a cold front ruffed the grass with shadows.

Margaret Hartley didn't ask again.
The eggs I'd found one by one
She stocked her empty basket with,
The prize one last. Everyone watched.
No one breathed.
                          Even the wind stopped. Dark
Turned the white dress Margaret wore dark too.

She and I stood alone,
There and in times to come,
Delicate hands taking everything away.
She wasn't Margaret anymore.
What could I do?
                          What could I say?

OHIO DREAM

You decide to come home.
You have only visited
Twice in thirty years.

It's been raining all spring
In Butler where you grew up.
Wind turns the water dark
Between corn rows.

As your near your old home
Sky brightens. Sun appears.
How important you think you are.
You have brought back light.

Days the sky dazzles.
Fields rearrange themselves in green.
Everyone is taking pictures.

But an old man in a house by the road
Stands at his window looking out.
He memorizes your movements,
Evenings your car coasting by.

He's sick. He can't work.
Soon he'll move away. In the VA hospital
In Marion he'll remember your coming.
He will hate you forever.

DEV AND ALICIA, THE SEQUEL

So there we stood, in starry Rio
Night, the mansion door closed
On our enemies, the road ahead of us.

We ought to have been happy, but you
Were already neglecting us. Oh sure,
You might have imagined us making love,

Maybe even slipped between our sheets
To find out if I liked women.
Let's say I've always cherished

Midnight drives along a coast,
The sea smell in a woman's hair.
How's that for an answer?

I'll tell you this, you forgot us.

I praise Alicia for trying to cook.
We dined out frequently.
Rio became a town we saw too much of.

I was posted to Washington eventually.
We mailed notices of our address,
But none of you bothered to write.

Our relationship ended quietly.
We disappeared from each other.
We'd become other people by then.

What did you expect?

1945–

15, tall and unhandsome, loner of
Oak shadows and gray fencerows, I
Worked the hay season stacking up
Bales on the wagons hooked behind
A rusty baler, hefting the twined
Grass with Frieda, our neighbor's
Son's brown warbride, who slicked
Water along her chafed bare arms,
And opened her army surplus shirt
To cool her breasts. She stroked
Them, drew her moist, salty life
Line across the ache of her skin.
In one whispered sentence, in her
Stranger's voice she said, Praise
The burning in us that elects us.

When the final day's wagon turned
Up the pasture's hill towards red
Barns and white silo slanted into
Evening, I slipped off, and I ran
Along the shore of an amber creek
Among cattails and willows, never
Stopping until I jumped the fence
And pressed my body down to lips,
Where the ground in the long corn
Rows opened to let out fragrances
Of loam, musk of roots and weeds.

Snake with a velvety, coal tongue
Coiled near my thigh then rattled
The dry cartilage of its tail; if
In joy or warning, I do not know.

TOURISTS

—You turn up at the oddest airports — she says.
We do. Like this one:

Sheds and hangers squat in the heat,
Shrines to lost lives, and the last plane
Is always disappearing in pleats
Of cloud. These archipelagoes

Exhale hyacinth and oleander,
Incense for the trade winds.
We nod, strangers who remember
Unpacking flesh to one another,

And once rising at dawn to sight
A solitary sloop rigged
Down wind through shafts of light
To chance the margins of the world.

We were afraid to follow. Lies
Sustain us, conscience our purest
Food. Duty always buys
Sleep and a ticket home.

Now when we meet we speak
Our blessings over the past.
We are the pilgrims who seek
Only our own ashes.

6 A.M.

Past my window
A crow is flying,
Wings dipping light.

The end of his flight
Is a hill beyond
My view, his essence
Is his flying.

But you, my child,
Who drops sighing
Asleep in my arms,
You will be told

Your essence is more
Than motion, is not
The flying in the cold
Days of this light.

One morning you will wake
With cold upon you.
Then all is flight.

THE FINDING

for Kimball King

One winter at the University of Wisconsin some women from a mental hospital were taken for a swim in the university pool. One of these women left the gymnasium and froze to death outside on the lake.

I

The doors were unlocked,
And so she left.
Then she was walking
Outside in the winter
Air which was empty
And blue. She hears
No voice she knows.
The giggling bodies
Go silent in the pool.

The boy is startled
By the naked woman,
And he shrugs deeper
Into his parka
And wonders what madness
Must send her out.

She passes the yellow
Bus that has brought

19

The swimmers. The sun
Is too thin to melt
The wedges of ice
In the corners of the windows.

She begins to feel
A burning in the tips
Of her breasts and inside
Her thighs. She rubs
Herself there and her fingers
Seem slowly to move,

As if belonging
To someone else,
Someone not there.

II

A face is watching.
A face so like
Her own, staring up.
And when she bends
Her face closer,
The other face
Changes and smiles.
The glass reflecting
Their smiles, the surface
Wide where the wind
Has blown away
The snow, and the blue

Inverted sky
Are drawing her down,
To kiss that face.

Her lips are chilled,
And she cannot speak
To this strange love.
But she senses something
Past coming near.
An earlier self
Forgotten, untouched,
Is waiting there
In the blue of an eye
And the smiling lips
Of another life.

Her swollen hands
Spread out and she falls
In the arms of a child
Who has died in the ice.

THE FINDING, II

Mama, she once said, between
my legs I am a cloud.

She was twenty then, but three
inside her head.

She died kneeling down
like she knew

a warm place she'd left
and was trying to see

her way back in again.
When I tell her story

I know who I am.

AN OLD IRISH WOMAN DEAD BY
FALLING GLASS FROM A HIGH RISE
IN BOSTON, MASSACHUSETTS

She knew.
She knew she knew,
Only she chose silence
And silence was the leaf enclosing the bloom
Across the winter portage between all waters,
Birth and dissolution. In the parks, no
Matter the season, she saw our spidery lifelines.

She knew.
But others found
Faith in glass geometries and numb reflections,
For we saw ourselves so endlessly repeated
We loved the glass greedily, forgetting
Bricks kilned from mud, chalked with our vanished masons' bones.

She knew:
Fear this city.
So her last day she stepped
Out in Celtic landscapes, where green descents slanted
Over old oaks. On the bright avenues, precise
As laboratories, she heard the beasts thrash
In their awakening. Ruin was always at hand.

The first
Pane fell softly,

Whining down like a dove
Stricken in a silent forest. At the severing
Of her skull a flower of blood burst across her throat.
One spectator said the shattering glass
Was like the twine of waves flashing upon an endless, windy shore.

BURIAL

They stand against summer
Trees glossed in slow light.

They have broken open the earth
To bury a gray bird that died this morning
Against the blue panes of the house.

Expecting to find only stones,
They have turned the plumage

Of another bird. Flakes of earth
Fall away. Oh, the birds are alike,

Each neck specked with brown
Blood, the same bone sprung
Through each gray throat.

They stand, this father,
This son, in disbelief.

Twilight comes on.
They dig another grave, nestling
The birds together. Overhead

The sky empties. Deeper
In the forest, already dark,
Leaves commence their chant,

Vines are changing shapes,
Serpents opening their eyes.

HILDA AND THE SNAKES

She followed them
Through fields where
She could not see
Them parting grass
And vines at the root.

She breathed the heat
Their skins left
On leaves or twigs,
Perceived the tarnish
On sparkles of mica.

Snakes never came
To her, and if
She pursued
One in the open
It whipped to strike.

We let her wander
The fields; we never
Hindered and only
Brought her back home
On rainy September

Nights, when she stood
Shivering by the orchard
And said, The snakes
Huddle for warmth;
They glisten and entwine.

THE WITCH

The wind off the Gulf
Convulses the palms,
Shatters the gardens.

In bed the lady
Dreams: a coffin
Floats down the air

Straight to her eyes.
They penetrate
The lid nailed shut.

She wakes; the name
Slips like an ash
From her lips. She packs

For another funeral.
Frail and ordinary
She rides the bus.

The family gathers;
They know her dreams.
None greets her, all

Refuse her claim
As blood and kin,
Her right to mourn.

She prays for this dead,
And she would pray
To die herself,

But for her dream
Of her blood transferred,
Throbbing in the stringy

Veins of the ragged
Owl who perches
On barn or house

Foretelling death
Upon death, clutched
By an unremitting force.

FOR HARDY, THE GARDENER

late the flowers
you pick for us

in October light,
gone gently summer,

fragrance lingering,
and arrange them,

purples, pinks, blues,
whites, in a vase upon

our table, blessing
us with them,

the late flowers
in October light

you pick for us,
gently summer gone

BURIED TREASURE

In nineteen twenty-seven, in New York,
A girl of nine trailing a taffeta robe
Passes her parents' door; the Sunday sun
Rouges the watchful shepherds on the wall.

Under the canopy airily arching
The winding finials of mahogany
Her father's hand rests by her mother's cheek;
Her mother's fragrance scents the rosy air.

The child descends the stair, careful to skip
The squeaky grain beneath the saffron runner.
The servants are not up; the only sound
Is of her robe rustling from room to room.

She stands before a fireplace; the dogs
Lap at her hem with iron tongues. She dares
To taste champagne caught in a crystal stem.
Then she bends down, draws back the edge of leaves

To vines woven, and lifts a stone from the hearth.
Out of her pocket she slips a milk-blue marble,
Strokes it upon her sleeve until the glass
Glows like a gem, shines like a sleeping face.

She gives her treasure to this hearth, and tugs
The stone into place.

FOR STEPHEN

Seventeen, no great event,
He says. He glides past us
With undisturbed intent.

He would photograph well
Easing into the jeep
Whose military shell

He painted red to cover
The old green wounds,
That war long over.

This boy, this innocence,
Brown summer muscle
Flexed without pretense.

There are no mysteries
For him. The winter branch
Always leafs into light.
His days shine with chance.

I follow his car in mine.
Dust rises from our road.
Three months without rain,
Already some of the pines

I planted a year ago
Are dead. When we reach

The highway, we go
Apart. Always the wrong time

To tell my son what I mean.
He doesn't see my wave.
When I was seventeen
I didn't look back either.

FISHERMAN

His back against the wall in late
Summer sun, he sits beneath
The Woolworth sign, jack-o'lantern
Face, he plays the wind with his teeth.

You avoid meeting his milky gaze.
He's too naked, too full of tricks.
I fish, I fish, he sings, and lays
Line and needle hook upon the air.

From slumber through winters of space,
Night by night he reels you in.
Cold pearls your eyes, and death your skin.
At his feet you plead for a saving grace.

TONIGHT

Tonight
to describe
the way the wind
lifts the willow branches

reminds me
of wind riffling
my father's hair

which is not to say
his hair was particularly long
or fine only

he died
and sometimes
words bless us

ROMANCE

One Thanksgiving in a northern
City, years before lawyers
Rearranged our lives, before
We settled up, I took a walk
Because the light was so
Revealing, alone, and the air
Temperate, out of season.

I came to an apartment building
Whose windows expressed many
Shadings between black and white.
Such marvelous balconies also
I beheld gazing up, allowing my
Self to imagine belonging there.
I saw a woman gazing down,
Inviting me.

I knew my wife waited
At home, cooking our goose
As it were, our kitchen
Ablaze with Revereware.
She would have changed into
A Bonwit cocktail dress.
I was in the Hathaway
Button-down, Bean twill,
And a blazer from J. Press.

The woman wore a long silver
Gown, completely wrong
For that time of day. Shadows
Suggested what she wore underneath.
The light was changing now.
The sidewalks were turning dark.
I was content to watch.
I loved words more than anyone.

MOBILE

I would like to believe.

I would like to believe
I am copper,
shining, spun
glistening a dark glow;
and older, like to believe
no patina will fret
brightness within.

I would like to believe,
whether waste or ornament,
among profusions of waste and ornament,
I would like to believe
I am suspended in a zone
of wind and mind —
    turned and turning
    in Christ's breath.

VESPERS

We are the spiritual junkies
Kneeling in the vesper light.

We gather each Wednesday.
None of us know each other.

We have bank accounts.
We dress in nice clothes.
We have portfolios of moral jitters.

We are the spiritual junkies.
We reach for the filling mystery.

The daylight behind us
Falls through the blue window

Of Elijah, who holds a brown hawk.
Over us the altar light is also on.

Our crossed hands make two shadows.
One darkest, and gray the other.

The priest floats the luminous body
Down our famished lifelines.
He bears the bright cup to our lips.

We are the spiritual junkies.
When we are fed, we stand.

We hold each other's hand.
The priest speaks a blessing.

Our hands are thin as leaves.
We feel the beating of each other's blood.
We are one. We are two. We are three.

THE REVEREND B.E. PALMER
CONSIDERS HIS HARVEST

February. Coldest armful of the year
To bear. The plow blade
Scrapes the path. No one travels.
Morning prayer I speak to stones.

But blessings on the post, its messenger
Of dreams deferred, who brings
The catalogue. I open to gravures
Of summer bounty: tomato, okra,

Kale, spinach, corn, broccoli, and
Cucumbers, yes cucumbers most of all.
I print my order neatly as a confession.

March. The seeds arrive. Outside I kick
Snow bonnets from twists of weed.
The earth won't give an inch.

April. I've paid my taxes. Daffodils
Curtsy by the path. I rake the ground.
A thousand disappointments nourish belief.
The dogwood petals flutter the Easter wound.

May. Impatient as a bridegroom
I open the packets, dab my fingers with my tongue.
The seeds cling to my fingertips. I press each
One by one into the earth like notes.

June. I order spices, count the jars.
July. The nation renews its vows.
Federal gardens proclaim the virtue
Of useful toil. I prefer disordered places.

Where seeds were planted, lamb's
Quarter, aster and brambles flourish.
Pollen buzzes around my wrist.

I feel the lifeline of prickly stems.
I feel until I find the first cuke.
Its skin is dimpled, delicate, confirming.
Slowly I tug others from the vine

And set to work making pickles.
Now, on this humid August morning,
I hold this jar of my labor before you.
Beloved, herein is more than meets the eye.

ROAD SIGN

Dear B.E., I dreamed I
Pulled off a road somewhere
To give this old person a ride.

Then I was driving again,
Music turned low. The old
Person wasn't chatty, rather

Thoughtful, I'd say, sitting
With hands clasped. Next time
I looked I found a form

Formed and reforming.
I asked, Are you God?
Sad eyes turned upon me.

I took that as a yes.
So, I inquired, of all
Our weaknesses and sin

What disappointed God
Most? Those Cubs,
God replied, they'll never win.

B.E., since you are my priest,
I pass this revelation on.
God could have said Red Sox.

FOR GEORGE YEATS, STREAKER

Dear George, while the old gang dries
To seed, puttering among regrets, or
Dabbles in Florida real estate,
Wonderful you are among us
Jumping out of trees.

At least that was the deputy's report.
You, once so pale and chubby,
Third string at everything,
Are charged with disobedience:
Naked in public thou shall not appear.

But those dim eyes who turned you in,
You leaping naked from the autumn
Bough, your heels scattering
Golden leaves, were not witnessing
George Yeats in a failed skin game,

But a sweet acrobat,
Your performance of belief,
You streaking into smoky light,
Giving nothing up, giving everything,
Glory lifting you on its tattered wing.

43

GRACIOUS LIGHT

I'm tired.
I haven't been outside
Myself for days.
Today is 12/21.
By 4 o'clock grayness
Tongues the house.

The clearing takes me off guard.
A glow through reefs of clouds
Widening down the valley, filling
The fields, chalking the sycamores.

I stand on the hilltop. Light
Palpable as wheat I cup
Into my hands. By faith I feed
Upon it. I hold on.

When my hands are empty
I go into the house again.
A few deer, almost invisible,
Ease along the fence row.
They are at home in darkness.
With help I make my way too.

JACKSON POLLOCK

in a photograph by Hans Namuth

The patches of grass around him
Are dry, as if all summer
No rain has eased the earth.
Beyond the pasture in which
He sits the trees become
The shadows. There is no wind.
There are no clouds in the sky.

He is looking at the grass
And not looking. He has
Come out of his studio and not
Come out. His eyes squint
With pain. His body is flexed
Like a boxer's, but he slumps down
To the dying grass. The cigarette
Burns at the tip of his fingers.

The watcher knows more than this.
There is a chance of rain
Which the moment does not suggest,
A wetness to soften the landscape,
A wind to move the trees.
Nature is unheroic.
Each leaf and spike of grass
Will reproduce its own self,
Or simply die without pain.

ON JACK'S BIRTHDAY

Thirty years ago you took me west.
Across that Wyoming summer snow
Fell forever one day in July,
Your birthday, Jack. The brush fires
Of the cowboys on the high range
Warmed our eastern skins.
On a swift palomino you chased
Mustangs through the canyons.

Thirty years. The winds have blown
Away the palomino's bones.
A thousand miles east of Wyoming,
In a room where whiskey warms us,
The snow lies deep upon your eyes.
You know me by the sound words leave.
I remember the slender aspens,
Jack, the trees of life you loved.

POEM

We are like moons. We live
in a thousand skies.
We are born out
of a narrow place.
We curve up-
ward. We
become
full.
We
are dead
though we know
not. We thin to
slivers. Fade. The sky
is empty. Gradually a speck
Appears, hard to find at first.

CHOSEN

I'm two, my crib crowds the wall.
We wait in rows to be squeezed and picked.
A new child rages in the hall.

He wants my bed, he wants my place.
Under the bowl of blue light
Shadows flicker across my face.

One day I'm brought a coat and hat.
In the back seat a woman says,
You're ours. She gives my cheek a pat.

I'm three. I sleep in an Ivory nest.
My new mother has forbidden me
To wet the sheets. My legs press

Together to do what I am told.
I shudder, giving the warm stream up.
Then I lie in flannel turning cold.

In the morning I shiver an hour
Smelling my skin in soiled pants
Before I'm ordered to the shower.

Water fills my throat. Stay there
Until you're clean, my mother says.
She orders the maid to scrub my hair,

Hands her the nub of soap, and disappears.
The maid lifts me out. She wraps
Me in a towel and dries my tears.

She dries between my legs, where nice
Boys never touch themselves. Be warned:
The doors of choice do not open twice.

I'm fifty-six. I dream blue light,
Siberian, desolate as love.
No one will choose me huddled tight.

OHIO, KNOX COUNTY, SEPTEMBER

On your left a mown field.
Two deer engaged with light lift
Their heads to hear your heartbeat.

On your right the breeze rustles tall corn
Squared in shadow. You imagine
A hand shaking a box of darkness.

You are standing on the floor of the world.
The paths pale up the hillsides.
Though trained in science, you

Remember nothing of wave theory
Or photons. Light and dark are
Absolute, the now, the then.

The deer thin into evening.
In the undertow of silence
Shadows are linking arms.

11/11

The weather was doing its November thing,
A windy light paling the grass.

My neighbors were doing a neighbor thing,
Forgetting to shut the gate to the pasture.

The horses discover the horse thing;
Out the gate they gallop up my hill.

My cat responds to horses circling the house.
The cat thing: pretend to be art.

I do the I'm from the city thing:
Approach the beasts, but no eye contact.

Finally the neighbors do the rescue thing;
They arrive with oats and bridles in their truck.

I do the let me try to help thing,
Leading one of the horses down the hill.

The horse does its I smell fear thing,
Jerking its head to make me let go.

Later I walk home. The wind stops.
A golden hush rearranges the pasture.

I disappear from myself. I see.
I am seen. The first thing. The last.

ETC.

This is what poems are:
Words going together
Back as far as
You remember.

Words knitting connection,
Perpetual resurrection.
Words to be sung
Even as the gas
Fills the lung.

Words of disorder
In order.
Words metered together
Syntaxed apart.
Words that break your heart.

Words slender as swans' necks.
Flighty as monarchs.
Juicy as littlenecks.
Tough as canvas.

Words rude.
Words nude.
Words pressed.
Words overdressed.

Words you read and put away,
Obsolete as beads on the stock exchange.
You cross the border one day.
You come to a village in the mountains.
The language you're accustomed to
Isn't spoken here.
You unpack the old words,
Primitive as flint,
Ripe as amber.
They guide you on your way.

Words that insist.
Give them to friends
Yet to exist.

Etc.

THE PLANNED CHILD

One overcast autumn morning in 1994 in Gambier, Ohio, I opened my post office box, slipped out an envelope, and moved to one of the old reading tables by the wall. There's not much in Gambier except Kenyon College. The post office was deserted, the students either attending class or sleeping late. On the wall above the table, its brown top stained with ink and scarred with initials, hung notices of lost animals, used cars, houses for sale by owners, and rides wanted. I opened the envelope and unfolded two pieces of paper: a birth certificate for someone named Roger W*** and a document that conveyed the court's permission for Roger W*** to be adopted by John (Jack) and Helen Brookhouse and his name changed to Christopher Brookhouse. Me. I was nearly fifty-seven years old, standing alone in a post office, discovering the people I had always thought my parents were not my parents, at least not my biological ones. I was excited, enlightened, and confused. My mind dashed everywhere. Faces sped by. One memory, a word, a place, rushed into another. I could stop nothing: no moment, no image, not even the faces of Jack and Helen. If someone had stood beside me, I would have stammered my discovery; but no one did, and I drove home and phoned my wife's office at the college. A few minutes later she hugged me, asked me if I was okay, and read the documents herself.

Receiving the news wasn't entirely a surprise. No civil servant atop a mountain of vital statistics hurled a bolt of enlightenment in my direction. I had filled out a request to

54

the State of Ohio for information about an adoption if one had taken place. The attorney for Helen's estate submitted my request. Helen had died two years earlier, a few months short of her ninetieth birthday. The clerk who received the request cautioned that records so far back (I was born in 1938) are often misplaced or lost. Two weeks later, however, the answer arrived from the Department of Heath in an ordinary business envelope, one of thousands like it sent out every day, routine and impersonal correspondence; but mine contained information deeply personal and long concealed.

I have no idea how many people knew I was adopted. Certainly, I had no intimation of it and disregarded, or delayed considering, the first clue that ought to have aroused my curiosity. In 1964 I won a summer fellowship to England. Although the donor wished to send Americans on a tour of English cathedrals, my faculty advisor in Harvard's English department told me to go to England and see what I wanted to see. Of course I needed a passport, and when I applied for one in Columbus, I was turned down. The clerk examined my birth certificate, or what I thought was my birth certificate, and pointed out it lacked a doctor's signature. Incomplete documents were not accepted. When I informed my father, he phoned his attorney, and I received a passport a few days later. My father, then in his sixties, a tall man with appealing brown eyes, a retired investment broker who respected privacy, his own and his clients', did not comment on the missing signature, nor did I expect him to. My guess was he thought the passport clerk had made a bureaucratic mistake and overstepped his authority. For my part, I neither examined the certificate to note the line where a signature was omitted nor checked for other omissions or information that might strike me as odd. I now realize I was incapable of noticing anything that might have raised questions. Anyway, what did a missing signature mean? Probably not much.

I left the rejected birth certificate in a desk drawer. Years passed. Sometimes the missing signature nagged at me, but by then I had two children of my own, and from my experience of doctors and hospitals, I knew physicians often keep the certificates to sign several at once. Skipping one in the pile wasn't unusual. So what troubled me? What was my question? Answer: had the clerk really made a mistake when he refused to accept my birth certificate? Did he misinterpret the rules or did he know them too well? And if I asked that question, wasn't I questioning the validity of the birth certificate myself? Wasn't I asking, *Are you my parents?* How disrespectful. How disloyal. Jack would be dismayed, Helen furious. I heard her saying, *Don't you love us?* Love to her meant loyalty and obedience.

Not until after she died (Jack had died ten years earlier) did I take another look at the bogus birth certificate. It was issued in 1940, two years after my birth. Nothing unusual, I reasoned. As a copy, a reissue, it bore its own date, not the original's. That my place of birth was listed as Cincinnati rather than Columbus, where my parents had lived until they moved to the house in the country where I grew up, would have puzzled me except for my recollection of Helen commenting that Jack had briefly worked in Cincinnati. Doing what? She didn't elaborate. Helen had always been much wealthier than Jack, and though she was proud of his professional abilities — he managed her investments and made her money — I sometimes felt her brief comments, asides almost, suggested she wanted me to see my place in terms of hers not his. Finally, there was the line on the certificate requesting the hospital's name if the birth had occurred in one. Another blank. My mother knew lots of doctors. She believed in them, and hospitals. She wasn't the sort of woman who would give birth anywhere else.

I phoned the Columbus Public Library. Someone located the 1938 city directory. The brokerage firm in which Jack was a partner was doing business in Columbus in 1938. Helen's remark about Cincinnati sounded less convincing. I filled out the form requesting adoption information, and Helen's attorney submitted it. He himself was skeptical. He had lived in Columbus all his life and, the son of the best man at Jack and Helen's wedding, believed if I were adopted he would have heard about it somehow: a rumor, a whisper, a remark overheard.

As Freud noted, children often deny the sexual relationship of their parents. I hoped to discover Jack and Helen had one. To characterize Helen as physically aloof, reserved, distant, is an understatement. She expressed herself in words, usually sarcasm, not by touch. I am sure she loved me, especially toward the end of her life, when by chance I had returned to Ohio and lived nearby and she depended on me. However, I recall only one time her touching me in a loving, tender way. I must have been eleven or twelve and suffered what people called growing pains. One evening when the soreness in my legs kept me awake, Helen massaged them with Absorbine Junior to relieve the pain. Once. Otherwise, I recall no embraces, and no kisses more meaningful than the perfunctory goodnight ritual of lips brushing cheeks. I never saw her touch Jack either, except one evening when they were very old and I found them holding hands as they watched the Republican convention on television. That moment of intimacy astounded me, and still does.

Jack and Helen liked alcohol, but cocktails encouraged no amorous behavior, only arguments, angry words as a substitute or protection against eros. Helen warned me about erotic inclinations and urges. Sex was dangerous. Sex was bad. Sex got you in trouble. I was probably thirteen when she casually mentioned that the man Jack sometimes spoke with when he visited an office downtown was her brother. My uncle! Apparently he had divorced his first wife, whom Helen admired, to marry a woman of dubious reputation, with whom he had been having an affair. To my knowledge, Helen never spoke to him again until, as chance would have it, the hospital where her brother lay in a coma asked her to see him and make a decision about his care. Helen agreed to remove him from life support. Eventually, she faced her own end with a similar directness.

Helen warned me about women. Some, particularly ambitious ones, were aggressors. Men, betrayed by sexual weakness, were their victims. Be strong. Do the right thing. When I headed west to Stanford University, Helen warned about the exotic seductiveness of oriental women. Although she had travelled around the world, I suspect her view of Eastern women derived more from the prejudices of American popular culture than from observation. By the time I left for college, she had disclosed the sexual mistakes of several fathers I knew and the effects on their families. Couples stayed together but lived apart. Husbands kept mistresses. Wives played bridge and drank too much. They spoiled their children. Heed the warnings. No wonder then that my first sexual relationship, begun my junior year with a Stanford classmate, initiated me into physical confusion, anxiety, and failure. As the years went by, I sought help from various therapists and browsed the growing number of books on sexuality to discover clues to my own sexual character. I became as compulsively drawn to statistics and analysis of performance as Helen was to the consequences of desire. In her declining years she suggested several of my contemporaries died from AIDS. In no case am I aware she was right.

By the time I turned fifty, I had achieved a degree of sexual maturity. In the year after Helen died, it wasn't sex that led me to consult a therapist again but a general, lingering level of anxiety about the midpoint of my life. The therapist pointed out how often I still heard and obeyed Helen's voice. The truth of the observation was obvious, overpowering. How could I have missed it so long? Doors opened. I walked through. I began to discover a self I had not recognized before. I emerged from the shadow of Helen's psychological power. In such a state of mind, I opened the letter from the Health Department. Presto, the biological basis of Helen's power crumbled too.

The names I read on the documents, my biological father's, my birth mother's, whispered more than sexual secrets. They gave me a connection to the past. I lacked any sense of family history. I had met Jack's parents (his father had been an insurance company executive) and liked them, but only saw them a few times before they died in the 1950s. Helen's were dead by 1940. I had little more than the names of Jack's and Helen's relatives. I had no family stories, no focus of family pride. Helen's father, a book salesman, had studied law privately and become an extraordinarily successful attorney, but she kept the details of his life to herself except to mention a few of his clients and once accompanying him to a courtroom in Chicago to watch Clarence Darrow.

In school I listened to stories of my classmates' families and longed for pioneers, patriots, inventors, entrepreneurs, no matter how distant or dubious, with whom I might claim a relationship. Jack once mentioned an ancestor decapitated by a cannonball in the War of 1812. I knew his family came from Salem, Massachusetts. In graduate school I frequently researched Jack's surname in the collections of colonial histories in Widener library and found several Brookhouses who qualified as patriots, sea captains whose adventures brought them renown. History interested Jack, but if I referred to the characters I had read about, his family, he appeared uninterested in them. Other than his unfortunate ancestor, he never mentioned another relative, not even his own parents.

Not having an historical sense of family is decentering. If Jack and Helen had decided to tell their family stories, I would have eagerly listened, and believed. Helen's silence struck me as hiding something. Perhaps Jack, urged by his conscience, wanted anything he told me to be the truth. Since I wasn't related to the people my research turned up, why talk about them as if I were? Helen's silence ultimately played a sad trick on her. After my wife helped Helen move into an apartment following Jack's death, she expressed great concern for a missing basket, one that I had seen many times growing up. Now she revealed that the basket had been carried to Ohio on her family's journey west in a covered wagon. Thinking the basket had no particular value to her, I had allowed it to be placed in the estate sale with the china and furniture she wouldn't have space in the apartment to keep.

FROM MY TRUE BIRTH CERTIFICATE I discovered my mother, probably of German heritage, attended a small rural college and was twenty when I was born. My father, probably of Irish descent, worked in a service station and was twenty-six. They were unmarried. I was born in a town in southern Ohio I had never heard of.

In the weeks following my discovery, I scarcely hesitated to reveal it to friends and acquaintances. All were interested, many deeply moved. My children, however, were neither. So wrapped up in my own life, I did not consider that my news threatened them with more changing family relationships. I was divorced from their mother and remarried; they had experienced one rearrangement already. Jack and Helen had been generous to them. Because I physically resembled my adoptive parents, my children found it hard to believe I was adopted at all.

So to the question people often asked, *Are you going to look for your biological mother?* my first answer was no. But in January on my fifty-seventh birthday, I realized that every year another person, a stranger, my mother, might have my birthday in mind too. I decided I needed at least to find out if she were alive or dead.

A friend recommended a genealogist in Columbus who traced missing heirs in cases involving wills and bequests. He quoted his fee (only a few dollars) and asked to borrow my true birth certificate. Two weeks later he supplied me with census reports giving more details about my family history as well as the address of my mother, whom he had located through a distant cousin of hers. A widow, she had, apparently, no living children. The report listed her father's nationality as German (the language spoken in the house) and his occupation as laborer. My biological father's family had moved to Ohio from Atlanta. His father made lasts for shoes. His grandfather had lived in Atlanta during the Civil War. I began to imagine two families and two people: an unmarried woman, my mother, had slept with a man and gotten pregnant. I was the result of all I had been warned about, sexual temptation, weakness, desire. Passion.

Such knowledge made me joyful. I welcomed it. By coincidence, I owned a 1937 Chevrolet, a car built the year I was conceived. I would sit in it and wonder if my parents made love in a car like mine, on a prickly mohair seat, or did they drive somewhere away from the campus and make love under an April sky, or in a borrowed room perhaps? I wanted — as Sharon Olds puts it in her poem "The Planned Child" — to have been "conceived in lust . . . by mistake, in love, in sex."

I couldn't get my mother out of my mind. I decided to write her a letter, tell her who I was, assure her I didn't wish to invade her privacy or upset her, express my willingness to meet but also my understanding if she didn't want to. Eventually, I received a phone call from her attorney. She had been utterly surprised, concerned, and uneasy at first when she read my letter, but she decided my words suggested a person of education and honesty and, on the condition my adoptive parents were dead, she would consider meeting me at some future time. He asked for additional information: what I did, where I had gone to college. I hedged, said I was a teacher, didn't say a writer. The attorney told me I would hear from my mother soon.

How honest was I? While carefully writing my letter, finding the right tone to express my intentions, I had chosen words sufficiently formal to put between us. To protect myself. How handy words are. The idea of making contact was one thing; to do it, something else.

Weeks went by. I expected a letter, none arrived. I thought she had decided not to see me. I didn't know she had been run over by a car some time earlier and was almost unable to use her hand to write. Then one spring afternoon the phone rang. I picked it up and my mother introduced herself. Could we meet at her apartment? She lived in an arranged care facility in Cincinnati. Because my wife wanted to go with me (I needed her to go with me) and her schedule was difficult since the college year was winding down, I proposed a day in June, a date far enough in the future not to be threatening at the moment. I wanted a few more weeks to savor what my imagination was piecing together, my story.

I was born in January, 1938, and adopted in November, 1940. I assumed I spent the intervening months in an orphanage. The representative of an orphanage in Cincinnati signed the adoption document. I began to blame certain behaviors on the traumas of orphanage life. I can't eat one cookie. I devour the box. Greed compensating for denial? Filling myself to assuage an old emptiness? The explanation is too pat, too simple, but sometimes it has resonance. I'm afraid of the color blue on maps. The blue on the top of the world disturbs me. Was there a blue sign, a light above a door in the corridor of the orphanage? I sense a line of beds: a hallway, footsteps, flashes of color: images from that long-ago life? Probably. My former therapist, now a friend, suggests traumatic memories stick; but not all orphanages produced traumatic memories, did they? When I meet my mother, I learn that I didn't spend all my time in an orphanage.

We meet outside her building on a hot, humid afternoon. I tower over her. She is thin, tiny, delicate. I soon notice our shared features: our eyes, the shape of our mouths, our hands. "You'll want to know how I could give you up," she says (did she say "abandon" or "give you up"?) and, seated between my wife and me in her apartment, she tells us. The apartment is comfortable, full of good furniture and knick-knacks from her travels. I notice, though, no photographs. She explains she was in love. When she became pregnant, her sister, a nurse, offered to arrange an abortion. My mother said no. I was born. She tried to keep me. She paid a woman two dollars a week to care for me, attended classes, and eventually received a degree and taught school. The beginning students. "It was the thirties. Illegitimate children didn't have much of a chance. Adoption was the only way. I knew it." She placed me in the orphanage and I stayed there for several months (how many my mother can't recall) until the adoption took place.

To PICK UP a relationship after fifty years is difficult, almost impossible. My mother and I have met other times and shared meals together and talked. I don't live in Ohio now, and we may get together once a year or exchange holiday cards. I think our first meeting, charged with so many emotions, marked in a significant way the beginning and the end of our relationship. We needed to talk, to listen, to see who we are, to hear who we were.

I don't believe my mother's closest friends know about me. I won't reveal her name here. I am a part of her life she wants to keep to herself. She married twice, both times to successful men, but I am her only child. She regrets she has no pictures to show me from her past.

Most of us in this century know our forbearers through photographs. We are the most photographed people on earth. I inherited several albums of pictures of Helen's family, going back to military men fixed in albumen prints in the Washington studio of Mathew Brady. Faces but no names. Strangers in a lost narrative.

In one of the photographs that Jack and Helen had of me, I am standing in a shallow, round washtub. I am chubby. The background is blurred, out of focus, but clear enough for me to know the picture was taken in a room I don't remember. My wife suggests it was taken by the woman my mother paid to care for me, and given to Jack and Helen by the orphanage. Pictures to interest them in adoption. Me, naked, looking at someone. I feel a deep affection for the woman in whose room I stand. In some buried memory her presence abides. I know she cared well for me. Perhaps loved me.

Love. That is what I am trying to write about. I love. I am loved. I will love. Except I hardly ever use the word. I'm not sure what it means, and I want it to mean more than "like," as in "I love peanut butter"; more than an expression of opinion: "we loved the movie"; more than what someone says to get something in return: "you know I love you." Love is what Helen was warning me about. In some deep way Helen had been injured or deceived or heartbroken. I know she feared and admired the power of her father. I know her mother died in an institution and such a fate terrified Helen. She wanted power herself and had it. She was cautious; the world was not a stable place. She depended on herself and the authority wealth conveys to those who have it. She was intolerant and overbearing. Yet she wanted to be protected and sheltered and cared for. She felt deeply but hid her feelings, though not her prejudices. She would express an opinion but never share her feelings, and sharing is one of the most important aspects of what, I think, love is. She did give away money. Financial gifts settled the emotional accounts, paid the fee that her conscience required in order for her repressed feelings to remain repressed, her emotional underground economy to stay in business. When she died, she willed a significant portion of her estate to a hospital that cares for children.

On the mantel in Jack and Helen's living room, in a gold-colored frame, was a tinted photograph of me, smiling, rosy-cheeked, at nearly the same age I was in the washtub, but certainly taken after the adoption. Jack and Helen immediately began to create a photographic record of me, their child. I'm scrubbed, dressed nicely, pleasantly posed. I'll admit I look happy in the picture, but I've always tended to follow orders well.

There are no pictures of my sister. At least I was told to call her my sister, a girl named Paula whom Helen brought home when, if I recall correctly, I was eight. She announced she was a year older. A room had been prepared for her next to mine. She lasted less than a week. Mostly I remember she gagged on toast and hid it in the register every morning at breakfast. When Helen found out, she demanded Paula eat the new toast served to her. Paula swallowed and threw up. She disappeared the next day. I think of her often. I still own the blanket chest Helen bought for her room. The bright veneer has faded and come loose. That's appropriate, I think. I can see under the surface, see through the work. I can see the rough edges that the builder thought would always be out of sight.

THE AUTHOR

Christopher Brookhouse was born in Cincinnati, Ohio. He received an undergraduate degree from Stanford University and graduate degrees from Harvard University. He has published three novels: *Running Out*, *Wintermute*, and *Dear, Otto*. *Running Out* won the Rosenthal Award from the American Academy of Arts and Letters. He is also the author of a book of poems and stories, *If Lost, Return*, and a previous collection of poetry, *Scattered Light*. He has taught at Harvard, the University of North Carolina, and Kenyon College. He edits *Hitchcock Annual* and presently lives in New Hampshire.